Everyday is Funday with Grandma Stella

A guide and memories keepsake for children and parents when a loved one suffers memory loss.

By Linda Ganzenmuller, Psy.D.
Illustrations by Susan Herbst

Published August, 2021

ISBN: 978-1-7376177-0-9

Library of Congress Control Number: 2021914889

For information address:
The Three Tomatoes Book Publishing
6 Soundview Rd.
Glen Cove, NY 11542

Illustrations: Susan Herbst
Cover and interior design: Susan Herbst

Tiny Professors is a trademark of Linda Ganzenmuller

Foreword

The best Alzheimer's care lies at the intersection of acceptance and creative problem-solving. It is the ultimate expression of unconditional love. That is the fundamental message of Dr. Linda Ganzenmuller's book. Based on years of practice as a therapist, she offers a unique perspective that is both personal and professional. Above all, Linda reminds us that the heart remembers even when the mind forgets.

As seen through a child's lens, *Every Day is Funday with Grandma Stella* demonstrates that connecting with another person means meeting them where they are. While that is always true, it's essential when it involves someone with Alzheimer's disease or another dementia disorder. Stella's grandchildren intuitively understand this. They make adjustments to join their grandmother's reality when it is grounded in a different place than their own. By extension, Stella is defined by her abilities rather than her deficits. The result allows a rich and meaningful relationship to continue even as cognitive challenges increase.

The book also includes a valuable opportunity to create a family legacy. Dr. Ganzenmuller's guide is filled with pages of helpful prompts to organize thoughts, feelings and memories. They serve to empower each participant by giving them a chance to tell their own story.

Dr. Ganzenmuller has my gratitude for carrying the torch lit by Mary Ann Malack-Ragona. The late founder of the Alzheimer's Disease Resource Center was a dedicated ally to those affected by Alzheimer's disease and other forms of dementia. That includes the diagnosed individual and those who love and care for them. Mary Ann was known for her practical, user-friendly approach which is beautifully evidenced here to be shared with all of you.

~Robin Marks, Executive Director of
Alzheimer's Disease Resource Center

Dear_____,

By now you know that I have something called dementia, maybe even Alzheimer's disease, which makes it harder for me to remember and understand things. Over time, it will probably be harder and harder for me to tell you all of the stories that I want you to hear, and all of the things that I want you to know. So, I'm writing them down now, so you can enjoy all of them anyway.

But first, there are some other really important things that I want you to know.

First of all, NO ONE caused me to be sick. That is just not possible, no matter what they might have said, or thought, or wished, or worried about. This disease just happened when my brain started to change, and there is nobody in the world who could make that happen.

Second, you need to know that just because I have dementia does not mean that you will get it, or that anyone else in your family will. It almost never happens that way, so you just shouldn't worry about that.

Third, you will probably be mad at me sometimes, or even embarrassed because I might say and do silly things. Then you might feel guilty for thinking like that. Don't worry. It doesn't mean that you are a bad person. It just means that something sad happened to you. I bet EVERYBODY will feel that way sometimes, not just you. The important thing is that we don't STAY mad, and that we try to help each other.

Fourth, there will always be people who can help you. If you feel sad, or mad, or confused, or if you have a bellyache or a headache, just talk to the same people you turn to now when you are having a bad day. Sometimes these people will have to help me a lot, and they will be very busy. Don't worry. They will always love and care for you, too.

You may have to ask them to help you. Sometimes, you may have to ask them a few times... and then a few times more!! But you should never be afraid to tell them when you need something. If you are having a really bad day, it might be a good idea to ask for permission to see your friends, or do something fun.

 If you are at school and you feel bad, you can always talk to your teacher, or the school psychologist or social worker. It might feel good just to talk, even if you can't make everything all better.

But here's the most important thing of all for you to know. We can still do lots of fun things together, and this book is going to give you some great ideas about how to do that. Even when it gets harder for me to understand things, you will be able to look at this book and get some brand new ideas, so that we can still spend time together like we used to.

I CAN'T WAIT TO GET STARTED!

Grandma Stella's been forgetting things lately and everybody's freaking out.
They're trying to fix *this*, and they're trying to fix *that*, and they're trying
to make everything better. But none of them know what they're doing.

If they were smart, they would just ask us. We know all about it.
That's why we always have so much fun.

She has something called Alzheimer's disease,
which makes it hard for her to remember and understand things.
People say she makes a lot of mistakes.
I say she's perfect just the way she is.

Mom and Dad worry when she doesn't know what time it is. They tell her to look at the clock, or look at the calendar.

We don't do that because it doesn't matter to us.

When we're together with Stella, we call every minute "great o'clock" and every day is "Funday."

And you know what? That never makes her worry, and it never makes her sad.

Grown-ups are so silly.

We used to play games all the time. She doesn't always know how to play them anymore, so we just make up rules as we go.

She finds the red cards, and I find the black ones, and when we're done, we mix them all together and start again.

Sometimes we play board games just to count the spaces. Once we went all the way around without stopping.

We do chores together, too. Mommy says Stella's house used to be perfect.
Perfect schmerfect!

We fold towels and no one cares if the corners don't touch.
When we're done, we high five because Mom and Dad are lucky
to have such good workers in the house.

People want Stella to be perfect. I want Stella to be fun,
because that's what I love most about her.

Mom and Dad say that Stella may forget how to do things like cook someday.
That's no good, because her cookies are the best.
So, I asked her to show *me* how to make them.

Someday I'll be "super baker" and everyone will come to me
for "Stella cakes" and "Stella cookies."

Don't tell Mom and Dad, but she's going to
teach me other secret recipes too.

Sometimes we take a walk together, and I ask her which flowers are her favorites, and which colors she likes best.

People are also saying that Stella might start telling stories that she believes are true.

They will want to stop her.

Not me! I think it's awesome.

We are great at make-believe, and I can pretend to be
in any story she makes up – as long as we are being safe.

And do you know the best thing to do when she forgets how to tell a story?
Ask her about when she was little like me!

People with Alzheimer's may forget things that just happened,
but they remember things from a long time ago.

That sounds crazy, but as long as I know that secret,
we'll have lots and lots to talk about.

Sometimes Stella doesn't understand me,
so I look right in her eyes and say things s – l – o – w – l – y !
Sometimes it works. Sometimes it doesn't.

But I never, ever let it make me mad.
She loves me and I know it,
so I'm okay when her memory is broken.

Stella says that someday she'll forget my name and may not
be able to talk to me at all. I can't believe it 'cause she loves me so much.
It made me really sad until she had a great idea.

She said she'd write it all down now so when she can't say it,
at least I can read it. That way, I will still know what she wants to say,
even when her words aren't working.

Stella is the best and she
ALWAYS will be. I'll make sure
of it, because that's exactly
how I will remember her.

The Story of You and Me

Dear Parents,
The following suggestions are a wonderful way for you and your child to gather memories from your loved one that your children will cherish for years to come.

Dear _____,

This is the story of you and me, just the way I hope you will remember it.

The very first time I laid eyes on you, I _____
_____
_____
_____ I will never forget what that felt like.

Right from the beginning, I dreamt of the days that we would _____
_____
_____
_____ and when you got older we did. Do you remember?

It was so exciting the very first time that you _____
_____
_____
_____
_____

I will never forget the time you made me beam with pride because you _____

_____

_____

_____

_____

You were so good at _____

_____

I used to wonder if someday you would want to become a professional _____

_____

When you were little, you really used to love _____

_____

_____

_____

and I loved watching how happy that made you.

I hope that you always remember the times when we would _____

_____together.

and when I taught you how to _____

_____

_____

_____

_____

Some of my favorite times with you were when we _____

_____

_____

_____

_____

Do you remember those?

We had nicknames for each other, too. You used to call me _____

_____

And I used to call you _____

_____

Sometimes, we just wanted to have fun together. I'll never forget how hard you made me laugh when you

_____

_____

_____

_____

_____

There were jokes that we would tell that were our favorites, like

_____

_____

_____

_____

_____

_____

One very special thing is that we were always good to each other, too.

When you were sad, I used to _____

_____

_____

_____

and when I was sad, you would _____

_____

_____

_____

and when we wanted the other person to know how special they were, we _____

_____

_____

_____

_____ I hope that never stops.

What are the things that you want to remember most? _____

_____

_____

_____

_____

_____

_____

_____

_____

_____

_____

_____

_____

_____

_____

_____

Those are all really good memories. But I want to make a lot more memories, too. Don't you?

There are lots of great things that we can still do together. You can look for fun activities online that help people with their memory. And we can always do arts and crafts, blow bubbles, play with clay, and even make up rules to our own crazy games. Why don't we buy crazy colored socks and race to fold the pairs together? Or listen to music, sing, look at old pictures, or read a book? Maybe we can even read THIS book together.

I think it would be great if we filled a box with things that remind us of times that we spent together. Sometimes, people put pictures in their box. Other times, people fill it with things that remind them of their hobbies, favorite music, or books they liked to read. Maybe we can even put in some of my old toys, or pieces to a game we used to play. This way, we can open it up together, and have fun remembering why those things are so special.

What do you think we should put in the box? _____

_____

_____

_____

_____

_____

_____

I will also put in my favorite recipes. Maybe someday you'll make them and think of me.

Which recipes do you like most? _____

_____

_____

_____

_____

_____

_____

_____

_____

_____

Someday, it may be hard for me to tell you all of these things that I want to tell you, so I'm going to write them down right now. More than anything else in the world, I want you to know all of the very best things about you.

_____

_____

_____

_____

_____

_____

_____

_____

_____

_____

And I want you to know all of the very best things about your family. _____

_____

_____

_____

_____

_____

_____

_____

_____

_____

And I want you to have the best life you can possibly have and be the best person that you can possibly be. So please take this advice:

When it comes to money: _____

_____

_____

_____

_____

_____

_____

_____

When it comes to love: _____

_____

_____

_____

_____

_____

_____

_____

When it comes to being a good person: _____

_____

_____

_____

_____

_____

_____

_____

Most important of all, I want you to know that, no matter what, my heart will always love you, even if I can't show it or say it.

So, I'm going to say it now.

I LOVE YOU NOW, AND I ALWAYS WILL. NO MATTER WHAT.

Love,

_____

MEET THE TINY PROFESSORS

Meet Kayla:
Age: 4 (a.k.a. "This many")
Nickname: Kayla–Bayla
Favorite food: Macaroni and cheese
Favorite thing to do: Color, and eat macaroni and cheese
What she wants to do when she grows up: Work at Disney World
Notes: She LOVES her grandma, especially story time and playing cards with her.

Meet Sebastian:
Age: 5 1/4
Nickname: Bassy
Favorite food: Pizza and macaroni and cheese.
Favorite thing to do: Watch or read anything about space
What he wants to do when he grows up: Go to Mars, or be an artist
Notes: He loves his grandma and loves asking her a million questions.

Meet Megan:
Age: 6
Nickname: Megeggan
Favorite food: Chicken nuggets and macaroni and cheese
Favorite thing to do: Play soccer, soccer, and more soccer
What she wants to do when she grows up: Be a soccer player
Notes: She loves her grandma and loves to bake and play games with her.

Meet Noah:
Age: 5 and two days
Nickname: Noah Lottastuff
Favorite food: Hot dogs and macaroni and cheese
Favorite thing to do: Build with blocks
What he wants to do when he grows up: Build the world's tallest and coolest skyscraper
Notes: He loves his grandma and loves when she gives him extra cookies when Mommy and Daddy aren't looking.

SPECIAL THANKS

I am grateful to Joan Motley for her advice, guidance, and support as I put this book together. Joan is a family liaison and care consultant and has been in the healthcare industry for over twenty-five years. She began to follow her passion for helping others by working under the assisted living umbrella and is now a highly regarded advocate for the aging population, especially for those with a cognitive decline. Joan has an extensive background in Alzheimer's Disease and related dementia and is a guiding force for those who find themselves in the overwhelming role as a caregiver. She provides the support that families require, through consultations and educational seminars that she has developed, relating to various important topics that empower the caregiver! Joan can be reached at Joan Motley Consulting, LLC, motleyjoan@yahoo.com.

ACKNOWLEDGEMENTS

I would like to thank my family for all of their love and support. Special thanks go to my daughter, Kayla Ganzenmuller, who helped me bring this story to life, and my daughter, Megan Ganzenmuller, who encouraged me when I really needed encouragement, and my husband Scott who made it all possible. I love you all so much for cheering me on and making this happen.

ABOUT THE AUTHOR

Linda Ganzenmuller, M.S., C.A.S. Psy.D.

As a psychologist, Dr. Ganzenmuller has worked in schools, private practice, and assisted living facilities. It was the time that she spent with senior citizens, many of them with memory deficits, that she learned her true calling. Her work soon focused on the elderly population, their children, and their caregivers.

Her years of experience have taught her the skills needed to develop safe and comfortable relationships with her patients, so that they feel at ease to speak openly about their concerns. Over and over again she has seen anxiety, depression, and frustration lessen, as interpersonal relationships have grown stronger.

Her insights have taught her that what people want and appreciate most is having their stories told, heard, and understood. That is why she helps her patients create written memoirs from the stories they collect, to be shared with family, friends, and professionals alike. These insights led her to create this book which is meant to be an invaluable guide on how to leave behind the legacy you choose for the people you love.

Linda earned her doctorate in psychology from Hofstra University, and continues her studies in aging, dementia, and the needs of her patients and their families. She lives on Long Island, New York, with her husband. She has two daughters, and together they all cared for her elderly parents in her home until their passing. She continues to work with adults in assisted living facilities, their homes, and in her private practice.

Linda can be reached at Supportive Psychological Services of Long Island, P.C., DrLindaGanz@gmail.com